TUBES IN MY EARS

My Trip to the Hospital

by **VIRGINIA DOOLEY**

illustrated by **MIRIAM KATIN**

To my wonderful family—Lou, Luke, Sam, and Nick—V. D.
For my parents—Klara and Laszlo Tobias—M. K.

ACKNOWLEDGMENTS

The author, illustrator, and publisher would like to thank the following people for their advice and help: Dr. David Bacha, pediatrician; Dr. Nancy Day, anesthesiologist; Dr. Miriam McKinney, Chairman of Pediatrics, Christ Hospital, Jersey City, New Jersey; Dr. Phillip A. Wackym, otologic surgeon, The Mount Sinai Medical Center, New York City; and Barbara Quinn, Assistant Director of Press Relations, The Mount Sinai Medical Center, New York City.

Printed in Hong Kong
96 97 98 99 00 01   9 8 7 6 5 4 3 2 1

Designed by Mina Greenstein
Production by Our House

Library of Congress Cataloging-in-Publication Data

Dooley, Virginia.
     Tubes in my ears : my trip to the hospital / by Virginia Dooley ; illustrated by Miriam Katin.
         p.   cm.
     Summary: A boy describes what happens when he goes to the hospital to have tubes put in his ears.
     ISBN 1-57255-118-6 (pbk. : alk. paper)
     1. Children—Hospital care—Juvenile literature. 2. Children—Preparation for medical care—
Juvenile literature. 3. Ear—Surgery—Juvenile literature. [1. Hospitals. 2. Ear—Surgery]
     I. Katin, Miriam, ill. II. Title.
     RJ242.D66   1996
     362.1'9892—dc20   95-39915
                                                                                     CIP
                                                                                     AC

Hi. My name is Luke. Did you ever wonder what going to the hospital is like? Well, I was in the hospital, and this is what happened to me.

It started last month. I got a bad cold. Then my ears really started to hurt. I knew I had another ear infection.

My mom took me to see Dr. Kim. She examined my ears and told me I needed to get tubes in my ears because I have so many ear infections. I thought she meant the kind of tubes you put in bicycle tires. Then she showed me what tubes for ears look like.

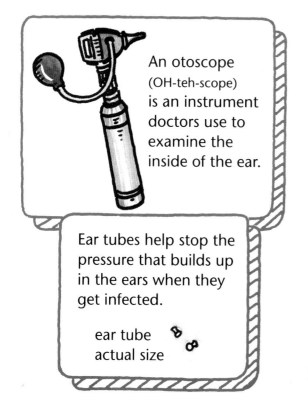

An otoscope (OH-teh-scope) is an instrument doctors use to examine the inside of the ear.

Ear tubes help stop the pressure that builds up in the ears when they get infected.

ear tube actual size

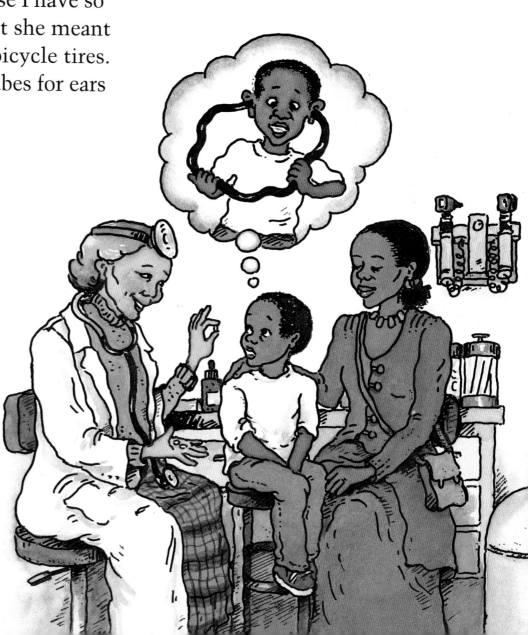

A week later, my mom and dad took me to the hospital to get the tubes in my ears. We had to get up really early. I wasn't allowed to eat or drink anything. I didn't even brush my teeth!

Not eating or drinking keeps the patient from throwing up and choking during an operation.

When we got to the hospital, we had to wait and wait. I was so hungry my stomach started to growl. I started to feel a little scared, too.

At last someone called out, "We're ready for Luke."

Next she took
my temperature.

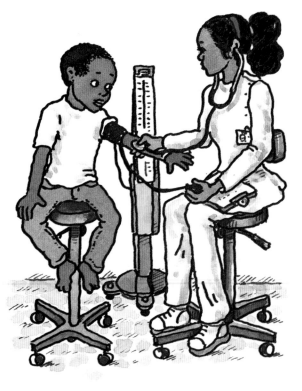

Then she wrapped a
band around my arm to
check my blood pressure.
The band squeezed my
arm really tight.

A nurse named
Claire weighed me.

Claire also listened to my heartbeat with a stethoscope (STETH-eh-scope). The stethoscope felt icy cold on my chest.

Finally I changed into funny pajamas with elephants all over them. They opened in the back and made me feel kind of silly.

Then I met Dr. Rivera. He told me he was an anesthesiologist. He explained that I needed to be asleep when they put the tubes in my ears.

An anesthesiologist (an-is-thee-zee-OL-eh-ist) is a doctor who puts patients into a deep sleep before an operation. That way they will not feel any pain.

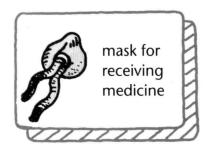

mask for receiving medicine

"Luke, would you like to breathe medicine through a mask or get medicine in a needle to help you fall asleep?" he asked. I picked the mask, of course!

Next Dr. Rice came in. He said he was a surgeon. He shook my hand. It made me feel very important.

"After Dr. Rivera helps you fall asleep," he explained, "I'll put the tubes in your ears. You won't feel anything."

Soon it was time to go to the operating room. I wasn't allowed to walk there, so I got a ride on a bed with wheels.

My mom and dad came with me. Dr. Rice told them they could stay until I fell asleep.

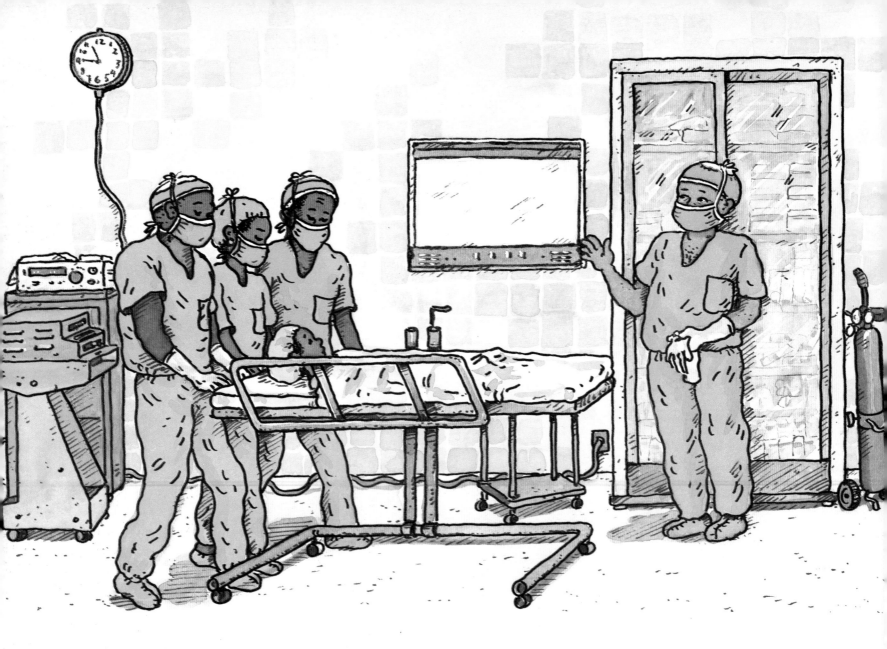

Dr. Rivera, Dr. Rice, and two nurses came
into the operating room. Everyone was wearing
special clothes and masks, even my mom and
dad. I started to feel a little scared again.

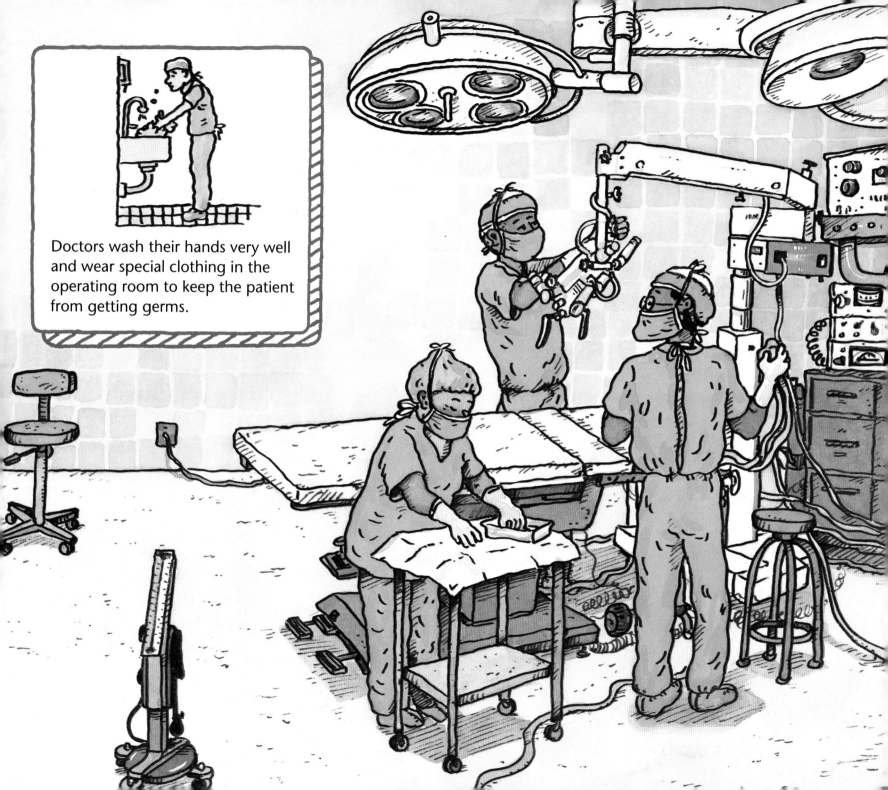

Doctors wash their hands very well and wear special clothing in the operating room to keep the patient from getting germs.

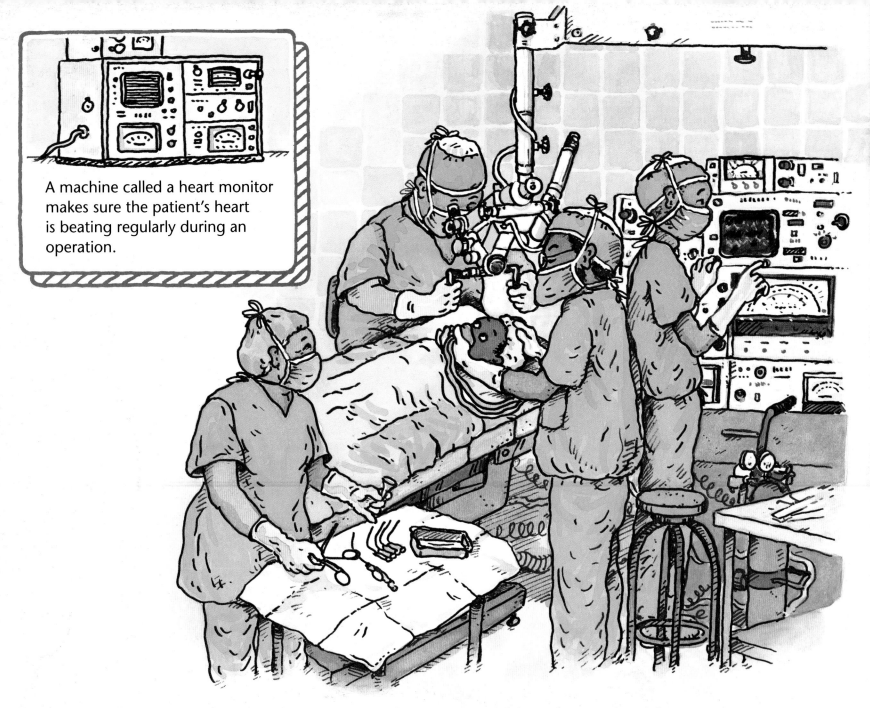

A machine called a heart monitor makes sure the patient's heart is beating regularly during an operation.

Dr. Rivera said everything would be okay. Then he put the mask on my face. He told me to count to twenty.

I started counting, "One, two, three-e-e, fo-o-our. . ."

That's all I remember.
I fell asleep before I even
got to five!

When I opened my eyes I couldn't remember where I was at first. Then I saw my mom and dad right by my bed. I knew I was back in my hospital room. I was glad the operation was over, but I felt sick.

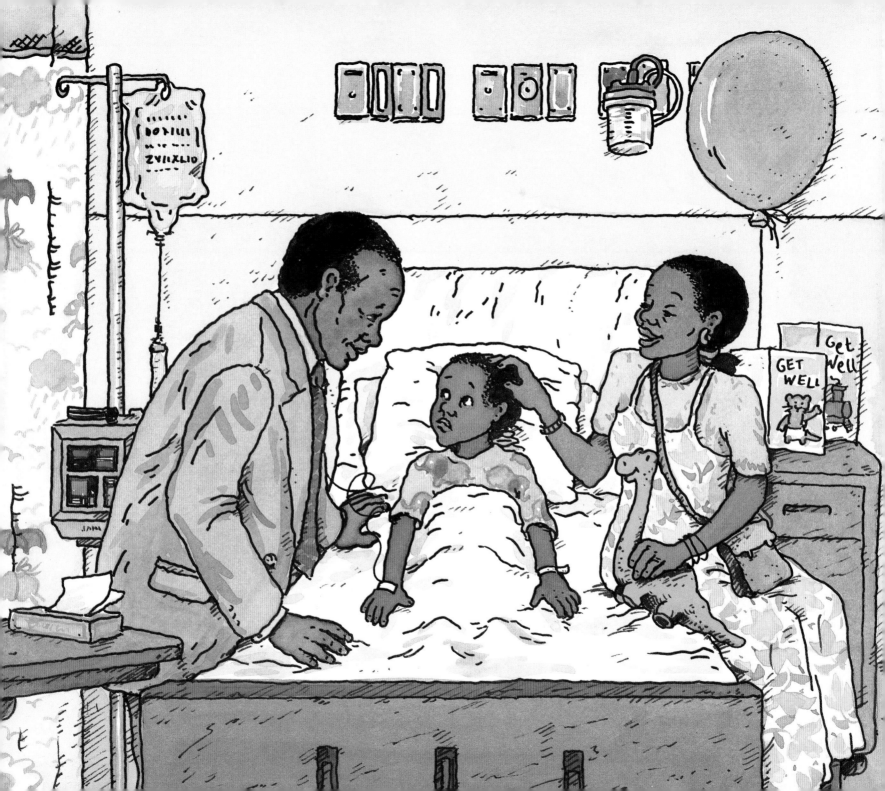

I had a tube in my arm. The nurse told me the tube was letting sugar water into my body to make me feel better.

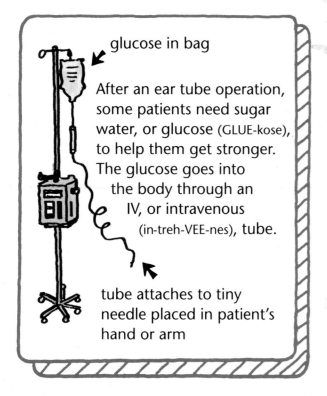

glucose in bag

After an ear tube operation, some patients need sugar water, or glucose (GLUE-kose), to help them get stronger. The glucose goes into the body through an IV, or intravenous (in-treh-VEE-nes), tube.

tube attaches to tiny needle placed in patient's hand or arm

But I didn't feel better. Instead, I threw up.
And my ears and mouth hurt.

Finally I felt good enough to drink some juice.
The nurse said if I drank a whole cup of juice and
didn't throw up, I could go home. I drank the juice
slowly to make sure it stayed down.

Dr. Rice came and looked at my ears. "You're doing great, Luke," he said. "You're ready to go home."

The nurse took the IV tube out of my arm. I got out of those funny pajamas as fast as I could. I was glad I didn't have to stay overnight.

Going to the hospital really wasn't so bad.
But going home was a lot better!